Eleanor ROOSEVELT

A Very Special
First Lady

Barbara Silberdick Feinberg

A Gateway Biography
The Millbrook Press
Brookfield, Connecticut

Published by The Millbrook Press, Inc.
2 Old New Milford Road
Brookfield, Connecticut 06804
www.millbrookpress.com

Cover photographs courtesy of © Leo Rosenthal/Timepix and Franklin D. Roosevelt Library;
Photographs courtesy of Timepix: p. 4; Franklin D. Roosevelt Library: pp. 6, 8, 9, 11, 15, 18, 28,
35, 39, 42, 43; Brown Brothers: pp. 13, 41; Underwood Archives, S.F.: pp. 16, 30;
Popperfoto/Archive Photos: p. 17; © Corbis: p. 20; AP/Wide World Photos: pp. 22, 27; ©
Frederick Charles: p. 25; Getty Images: pp. 33, 36

Library of Congress Cataloging-in-Publication Data
Feinberg, Barbara Silberdick.
Eleanor Roosevelt : a very special first lady / Barbara Silberdick
Feinberg.
p. cm. — (A gateway biography)
Summary: Introduces the wife of President Franklin Delano Roosevelt and
U.S. delegate to the United Nations.
Includes bibliographical references and index.
ISBN 0-7613-2623-5 (lib. bdg.)
1. Roosevelt, Eleanor, 1884-1962—Juvenile literature. 2. Presidents'
spouses—United States—Biography—Juvenile literature. [1. Roosevelt,
Eleanor, 1884-1962. 2. First ladies. 3. Women—Biography.] I. Title.
II. Series.
E807.1.R48 F45 2003
973.917'092—dc21   2002003413

Eleanor ROOSEVELT

TIME

THE WEEKLY NEWSMAGAZINE

Thos. D. McAvoy

ANNA ELEANOR ROOSEVELT

The scrambled world has superseded scrambled eggs.

(National Affairs)

Eleanor Roosevelt appeared on the cover of Time *magazine three times—in 1933, 1939 (shown here), and 1952.*

A Proper Young Lady

Anna Eleanor Roosevelt was born on October 11, 1884, in New York City. Everyone called her Eleanor. She had two younger brothers: Elliot Junior and Hall. Elliot was born in 1889 and Hall was born in 1891.

Eleanor's parents were Anna Hall and Elliott Roosevelt. They both came from wealthy New York families. Eleanor's uncle, Theodore Roosevelt, was president of the United States from 1901 to 1909.

Anna didn't think Eleanor was pretty. She had blue eyes and long, thick, blond hair, but her beautiful mother thought she was plain. Anna told her, "You have no looks. So see to it that you have manners." Eleanor wrote that she "wanted to sink through the floor in shame" when her mother described her as "a funny child, so old-fashioned that we always call her 'Granny.'"

Eleanor's mother called her "Granny" because even as a little girl she sometimes acted like a much older person. Her father liked to call her "Nell," after the character in Charles Dickens's Old Curiosity Shop, little Nell.

Eleanor loved her father, but he wasn't a good dad. Once they walked their dogs to his club. He went inside for a drink, leaving Eleanor with the doorman. Six hours later, the doorman sent her home in a cab. Her father's friends had already taken him home because he was very drunk. He had a problem with drinking alcohol.

Eleanor could tell that her parents did not get along, but she did not know why. By the time Eleanor was six, her father was away most of the time. Alcohol made him violent, and he didn't want to hurt his family. Eleanor tried to help her sad mother. She rubbed Anna's head for hours, trying to make her headaches go away. She said: "The feeling that I was useful was perhaps the greatest joy I experienced."

The years 1892 to 1894 were especially hard for Eleanor. First, her mother died of a disease called diphtheria, a serious throat infection. Her father came to the funeral. Eight-year-old Eleanor was so happy to see him that she hardly cried for her mother. He didn't stay because he could not take care of his children. He visited sometimes and wrote letters to Eleanor.

Eleanor and her brothers went to live with their Grandmother Hall. A year later, baby Elliott died of scarlet fever and diphtheria. The next year Eleanor's

Elliott Roosevelt with his daughter Anna Eleanor, and two sons, Gracie Hall (called Hall) and Elliott Junior in 1892. Elliott died in 1893.

father died because he could not stop drinking alcohol. It poisoned him. When Eleanor heard he had died, she "simply refused to believe it." She cried and cried. Grandmother Hall didn't let the children attend his funeral because they were too young. Eleanor often daydreamed that her father was still alive.

Eleanor and Hall lived with their grandmother in New York City and at Tivoli. Tivoli was her big house overlooking the Hudson River. Grandmother Hall didn't think she had been strict enough with her own children. So she was strict with Eleanor and Hall. "We were brought up on the . . . [idea] that 'no' was easier to say than 'yes.'" Eleanor didn't really mind. She was the center of attention for the first time in her life. She enjoyed it.

Eleanor at Tivoli with one of her family's horses. She conquered her fear of horses to become a good rider.

Her grandmother took charge of Eleanor. She hired teachers for her granddaughter. Lots of wealthy people did this. She even picked out clothes for her. Eleanor's cousins and friends teased her for wearing such old-fashioned, ugly dresses.

Worried about Eleanor's posture, her grandmother made her wear a steel brace for a year. She thought it would help straighten Eleanor's spine. Yet she refused to have braces put on Eleanor's front teeth even though they stuck out. Grandmother Hall did not believe young ladies should have their teeth straightened.

She taught Eleanor some valuable lessons. One thing she taught was that you should help people who don't have as much as you do. So Eleanor visited poor sick babies in the hospital. She felt a strong sense of duty toward others. Another lesson Eleanor learned was to keep promises to other people. If she agreed to go to a party, she had to show up, even if she did not feel well.

When Eleanor was fifteen, her grandmother sent her to Allenswood, a boarding school in England. A French woman named Marie Souvestre was in charge. She didn't like some of the things Eleanor's grandmother had taught her. Souvestre told Eleanor she should think for herself. Instead of hiding her feelings, she told Eleanor to show her emotions. Souvestre also helped Eleanor pick out new clothes that looked better on her tall body. Eleanor was five feet nine inches tall.

Eleanor studied English literature, German, and music. She was not the best student in the school but other girls looked up to her as a leader. For holidays, Souvestre took Eleanor on trips to other countries. She even gave her a guidebook and let her go off by herself in strange cities. Sometimes she asked Eleanor to plan their trips. This made Eleanor feel more capable and useful. She loved to travel.

After three years at Allenswood, Eleanor went home to New York. She was eighteen. Grandmother Hall wanted eighteen-year-old Eleanor to make her debut.

Allenswood school near London, England, where Eleanor's friends called her "Tottie."

This meant meeting lots of new people at parties, teas, and dances. Going to these events was a way for young women to show they were ready to get married.

Eleanor's old teacher, Miss Souvestre, helped Eleanor get ready for her debut. Souvestre knew it wouldn't be all fun and games. She wrote: "There are more quiet and enviable joys than to be among the most sought-after women at a ball or the women best liked by your neighbor at the table, at luncheons and the various fashionable affairs." Eleanor appreciated her advice.

A Respectable Wife and Mother

Eleanor spent her first winter back in New York going to teas and dances. She wrote: "I was the first girl in my mother's family who was not a belle." She felt awkward around her cousin Alice, President Theodore Roosevelt's daughter. Alice was witty and popular. She made fun of Eleanor for being too proper, serious, and shy.

Yet Eleanor began to look forward to the dances where her fifth cousin, Franklin Delano Roosevelt, turned up. Franklin was two years older than Eleanor and a student at Harvard University. He lived with his widowed mother, Sara, at Springwood near Grandmother Hall's Tivoli. Eleanor and Franklin had met as children. Now

Eleanor's fifth cousin Franklin Delano Roosevelt

he often took her to parties. He praised her to his mother, saying, "Cousin Eleanor has a very good mind."

Remembering her grandmother's lessons, Eleanor did volunteer work. She visited dark, airless factories and told the Consumers' League about terrible working conditions. She went to the Rivington Street Settlement House as a member of the Junior League. This was a place that helped people new to America become citizens. It was on the Lower East Side of Manhattan. It was an area with "foreign-looking people" and "filthy streets," according to Eleanor. She taught children exercises and dancing. Franklin often met Eleanor at Rivington Street and took her home. He worried about her safety.

In 1903, Franklin asked Eleanor to marry him, and she said yes. Sara Roosevelt thought her son was too young to marry. She made the couple promise to wait a year and keep their engagement a secret. Eleanor wrote to Franklin: "We must both try always to make her happy & I do hope someday she will learn to love me." Sara took Franklin on a cruise to the Caribbean, hoping to end the romance. She failed. In October 1904, Franklin gave Eleanor a ring.

Their wedding was on March 17, 1905, at the home of one of Eleanor's cousins. Her uncle Theodore, still presi-

*At her wedding, Eleanor wore her mother's wedding dress,
her grandmother's lace veil, and a pearl necklace
from Sara Delano Roosevelt.*

Theodore Roosevelt was president when Eleanor got married, so he got more attention from the guests than Eleanor and Franklin.

dent of the United States, gave the bride away. At the end of the wedding, President Roosevelt slapped the groom on the back and said, "Well, Franklin, there's nothing like keeping the name in the family!"

Eleanor and Franklin went to Hyde Park for a week as their honeymoon. Then Franklin returned to Columbia University to study law. When school ended for the summer the newlyweds went to Europe. There they enjoyed the sights and visited with friends and family.

When they got home, they found that Sara had rented a house for them. She had also bought furniture and hired servants. She wanted to take charge of their lives.

Sara Delano Roosevelt, Franklin's mother, tried to take charge of Eleanor's life, but Eleanor slowly began to make decisions for herself.

In 1908, Sara bought twin homes for the young Roosevelts and herself. She had sliding doors put in on each floor to connect the two buildings. The couple also spent summers with her at Hyde Park and at Campobello, an island off the coast of Maine. Because she wanted Sara to love her, Eleanor followed Sara's rules.

Eleanor wrote: "For the next ten years I was always just getting over having a baby or about to have one." She gave birth to six children: Anna Eleanor in 1906; James in 1907; Franklin Jr. in 1909; Elliott in 1910; another Franklin Jr. in 1914; and John in 1916. The first Franklin Jr. had a weak heart and died when he was seven and a half months old. Eleanor was sad for a long time.

Franklin and Eleanor with their children Anna, James,
John, Elliott, and Franklin Jr., and Sara Roosevelt
in Washington, D.C., in 1920.

Sara hired nursemaids and governesses to take care of the children. Sara told Eleanor to give up her volunteer work. She feared that Eleanor might bring nasty germs home and make the children sick. Eleanor listened to her mother-in-law. However, she was hurt when Sara competed with her for the children's love.

To fill her day, Eleanor wrote: "I did a great deal of embroidery during these years, a great deal of knitting, and an amount of reading. . . ." Eleanor also went to teas and other social functions as Sara wanted.

In 1910, Franklin became a New York state senator. The young Roosevelt family moved to their own house in Albany, the state capital. Sara didn't visit very often. She didn't like politics. Eleanor ran her own house and hired her own staff. She liked meeting people and learning about political issues.

In 1913, President Woodrow Wilson made Franklin an assistant secretary of the navy. The Roosevelts moved to Washington, D.C. Eleanor had to visit the wives of other government officials. She hired a young social secretary, Lucy Mercer, to help her keep up with her mail and reply to invitations. The two women grew close.

In 1917 the United States entered World War I to fight Germany and Austria. Eleanor knitted for the soldiers.

Lucy Mercer

She also helped organize Red Cross canteens that met troop trains and handed out snacks.

Franklin went to Europe in 1918 and returned home sick with pneumonia. Eleanor unpacked his luggage and sorted his mail, finding love letters from Lucy Mercer.

Eleanor told Franklin she would give him a divorce. In those days, the public did not accept divorce. Sara insisted that the couple stay together. She threatened to cut her son off without a cent if he left Eleanor. Ending his marriage would have ruined Franklin's political career.

Eleanor chose to forgive Franklin, but she also set about building a life of her own. No longer would she accept Sara's rules or lead the life of a society woman. She said: "The bottom dropped out of my . . . world, and I faced myself, . . . my world, honestly for the first time. I really grew up that year."

A Successful Career Woman

The first year American women could vote for president was 1920. Eleanor joined the League of Women Voters, a group that helped women learn about elections and voting. Also, she worked in Franklin's campaign. He was the Democratic party's candidate for vice president. (James M. Cox, governor of Ohio, was the Democratic presidential candidate.)

Eleanor traveled across the country with Franklin by train. She felt lonely and bored on the trip. She had to sit on platforms and listen to her husband give the same speech in town after town. Then his adviser, Louis Howe, began to ask Eleanor what she thought of Franklin's speeches and other issues. He brought reporters to meet her. She wrote: "I was flattered and before long found myself discussing a wide range of subjects." When the Democrats lost the election, Eleanor took business classes. She also learned to cook.

In 1921, tragedy struck during a family vacation on Campobello Island. Franklin became sick with polio and lost the use of his legs. (This was before the discovery of a vaccine against the disease.) The Roosevelts moved back to New York. Their house was crowded with the children, Franklin's nurse, and Louis Howe, as well as

Franklin with his dog, Fala, and Ruthie Bie, granddaughter of the caretakers at Hill Top Cottage near Hyde Park. After he had polio in 1921, Franklin used a wheelchair most of the time. However, he wanted to look capable and strong, so he was rarely photographed in his wheelchair.

Franklin and Eleanor. Sara told Franklin he should retire to Hyde Park and give up politics because he was sick. Eleanor disagreed.

The pressure of dealing with her sick husband, the children, the house, and her mother-in-law, became too much for Eleanor. One day, she burst into tears while reading to Franklin Jr. and John and could not stop crying. "This is the one and only time I remember in my entire life having gone to pieces. . . ."

Louis Howe and Eleanor didn't want Franklin to retire. Howe talked Eleanor into doing political work. This kept Franklin interested in current events. It also kept people from forgetting him. At first, Eleanor had trouble making speeches. Her high voice and nervous giggles distracted the audience. Howe worked with her. He helped her feel more comfortable speaking in public.

Eleanor joined the Women's City Club of New York. The club wanted to make the city a better place to live. She led committee meetings, urged people to pay their dues, and ran errands.

Eleanor wanted to make life better for women. She worked to shorten the workday for women and to end child labor. She helped set up health care clinics for mothers and children. She also spoke out against war and wrote antiwar articles for a newspaper called *Women's Democratic News*.

Eleanor made friends with schoolteacher Marion Dickerman and her friend Nancy Cook. The three women had picnics near Val-Kill Stream in Hyde Park. Franklin let them build their own cottage on three acres of land. In 1925, Val-Kill Cottage was ready. It was Eleanor's first real home. She hadn't really felt welcome at Hyde Park. At Hyde Park, Sara was the head of the house, not Eleanor or Franklin. Now Eleanor would not have to ask Sara if she wanted to have her friends visit.

The three women started a furniture factory called Val-Kill Industries in 1927. They hired farmers and young people in the Hyde Park area. At the same time, Eleanor started teaching at the Todhunter School in Manhattan. She taught American history, English, and American literature. Eleanor, Marion, and Nancy bought the school and ran it themselves. Eleanor also wrote articles for women's magazines. She gave the money she earned to projects she believed in, like Val-Kill Industries.

Eleanor had lots of energy. She continued doing most of these things and added more when Franklin became governor of New York state in 1928. (He was reelected in 1930.) Franklin sent Eleanor all around the state as his eyes and ears. This was because he could only walk with

Eleanor built a cottage and a factory near Val-Kill stream in New York as a home and business of her own.

crutches and metal braces. He trained Eleanor to be a good observer. For example, when she visited a state hospital, she did not just read the menus, she also looked into the pots to see what was cooking.

Just after Eleanor's forty-fifth birthday, the stock market crashed. Stocks that people owned in corporations lost almost all their value. Many businesses closed, putting people out of work. The government didn't do anything to help hungry, homeless Americans. States and private charities ran out of money. People were ready for a change, so they elected Franklin D. Roosevelt as president in 1932.

Eleanor was not happy about becoming the First Lady. "I was deeply troubled. As I saw it, this meant the end of any personal life of my own. . . . I had watched Mrs. Theodore Roosevelt [Aunt Edith] and had seen what it meant to be the wife of a president, and I cannot say I was pleased at the prospect."

Eleanor was not sure she could keep working on the projects that interested her. To do so she changed the job of First Lady. She made the job fit her needs.

A New Kind of First Lady

Eleanor Roosevelt was not like other First Ladies. She moved the furniture in the White House on her own. She surprised the staff by running the elevator herself. She refused Secret Service guards and drove her own car.

Eleanor was the first First Lady to hold regular press conferences. She only let female reporters come. She wanted to help them keep their jobs in a time when it was hard for anyone to find work.

Other First Ladies were just hostesses, but Eleanor kept working. Although she gave up teaching, she still wrote, gave lectures, and hosted a radio program. In 1936 she even started a newspaper column, called "My Day." It told people about what she did as First Lady and about her other interests. Newspapers ran that column until 1962 when bad health forced Eleanor to stop writing.

Critics said that being First Lady was a full-time job. Eleanor replied, "What some people do not seem to understand is that I am really not doing anything that I haven't done for a long time. It's only Franklin's position that has brought them to the attention of people."

Eleanor with Amelia Earhart, a famous pilot, in 1935. Eleanor loved to fly, and she made air travel acceptable to the public. Eleanor and Amelia once flew over the Capitol at night with Eleanor, dressed in an evening gown, at the controls.

Franklin and Eleanor at the White house

Eleanor had enough energy to take on a very busy schedule. She went horseback riding every morning at seven. Then she had breakfast at eight-thirty, usually with guests. After that, she took care of First Lady chores like choosing menus and making seating plans for official dinners. She hired a housekeeper to take care of the White House. After lunch with guests, she worked with secretaries to answer mail and plan her schedule. (She received 300,000 or more letters in 1933.) Eleanor sometimes shook hands with one thousand people a day at afternoon receptions and teas.

She invited people to dinner that she wanted her husband to meet. She tried to convince Franklin to support projects that were important to her. Sometimes he just wanted to relax, but she urged him to take action. For example, she asked him to fund a camp for jobless young women. Young men already had Civilian Conservation Corps (CCC) camps, where they planted trees and helped protect the environment. She usually wrote her newspaper column just before bedtime, often after midnight.

Touring the country for her husband, Eleanor drew attention to people and problems. She was the first wife of a U.S. president to testify before a congressional committee. She told members of the Tolan Committee about the problems of workers who traveled from state to state to harvest crops.

Eleanor wanted to solve all the problems she saw. In 1933 and 1934, she helped create Arthurdale, in West Virginia. It was a place for jobless miners and their families to live. It had cheap housing, land they could farm, and factories where they could work. Eleanor often vis-

Eleanor traveled all over the country. She once went into a coal mine to see what the working conditions were like. Some people thought she should stay home and take care of the White House. Others liked to know that she cared enough to see what their lives were like.

ited to inspect the town. She hired workers and raised money. This project and others like it didn't work out very well. Eleanor learned that "there is always grave danger in anything that is experimental. One must not do too much for people, but one must help them to do for themselves."

Eleanor also cared about America's young people. Often they could not find jobs and did not have the money to go to college. In 1935 she convinced the government to set up the National Youth Administration (NYA). This agency gave part-time jobs to students and young adults. She was also interested in the American Youth Congress (AYC), a radical reform group. She supported them until they began to hold beliefs that were hurtful to the United States.

The problems of African Americans troubled Eleanor. Laws and local customs forced them to live apart from white Americans. There were separate schools, buses, lunch counters, playgrounds, and movie theaters for whites and blacks. Eleanor tried to convince her husband and his staff to do more to help. She often invited African-American leaders to the White House. She wanted laws passed to protect blacks from being killed by angry white mobs. She also tried to get blacks more jobs.

In 1939 the Daughters of the American Revolution (DAR) refused to allow black opera singer Marian Anderson to perform in their Constitution Hall in Washington, D.C. Eleanor wrote in her newspaper column: "To remain as a member implies approval of that action, and therefore I am resigning." She helped arrange for Ms. Anderson to sing at the Lincoln Memorial.

In 1939 war broke out in Europe, and Japanese armies marched against European colonies in the Pacific. Eleanor invited the visiting king and queen of England to a picnic with hot dogs and cold cuts at her Val-Kill cottage. This informal meal shocked her mother-in-law but delighted the guests. The royal visit was the first of many between British and American leaders during the war.

Eleanor tried to get the United States to admit more refugees from Europe. Germany was rounding up its Jews, using them as slave labor, and killing them. Yet, some Americans feared that Jewish refugees would take away their jobs or would spy on them for foreign nations. Others hated Jews. In 1938, Eleanor wrote: "This German-Jewish business makes me sick."

No First Lady before Eleanor had ever given a speech at a national political convention. (This group of politicians from all the states meets every four years to choose their party's candidate for president and talk about issues.) In 1940, however, Franklin sent his wife to talk to the Democratic National Convention in Chicago.

The politicians were willing to nominate Franklin for an unheard-of third term as president. Eleanor had to convince them to accept Roosevelt's choice for vice president, Henry Wallace. She said: "This is no ordinary time. . . .

At the Democratic convention in California in 1940,
Eleanor gave a speech asking people to elect
Franklin for a third term as president.

No man who is a candidate or who is President can carry this situation alone."

The year 1941 was a difficult year for Eleanor. On September 7, 1941, Sara Delano Roosevelt died. Eleanor wrote: "I kept being appalled at myself because I could not feel any real grief." However, on September 25, she felt very sad when her brother Hall died. Like his father, he had become an alcoholic, and Eleanor was angry that he had wasted his life. "I think it was in an attempt to numb this feeling that I worked so hard at the Office of Civilian Defense [OCD] that Fall."

A few days before she lost her brother, Eleanor had become the first First Lady to accept a government job. She worked at the OCD as an unpaid assistant director. Her job was to focus on civilian morale, medical care, and housing. Just three months later, on December 7, Japan attacked the American naval base at Pearl Harbor, Hawaii. The United States went to war.

Members of Congress didn't like the way Eleanor did her job at OCD. They said she gave jobs to people they thought were disloyal to the United States and people who didn't want to serve in the military. They said she was disobeying laws separating the races when she gave jobs to African Americans in the South. Their comments

were so nasty that she quit
her job on February 20,
1942, to protect the agency.

Eleanor traveled a lot
during the war. She went
to England in 1942. She
watched what British
women did to help the war
effort. Then she visited
camps in Arizona where
Japanese Americans were
held under guard. She was
upset that Americans
"knew so little and cared
so little about them."

Eleanor's four sons were
in the armed forces. She
did what she could for
other wartime mothers.

*During World War II, Eleanor went
to Bora Bora to meet with the soldiers who were living there. She also
went to Guadalcanal, Hawaii,
Christmas Island, Samoa, Fiji,
New Zealand, and Australia.*

She visited American soldiers and took messages back to
their loved ones. In 1943 she went to the southwest
Pacific to inspect Red Cross posts and military bases.
The next year she visited soldiers and sailors in the
Caribbean.

In 1944, Franklin decided to run for a fourth term. "I dread another campaign, and even more another 4 years in Washington, but since he's running for the good of the country I hope he wins," Eleanor wrote to a friend.

While Eleanor was away, Franklin began seeing Lucy Mercer (Rutherford) again. She was a widow now. Lucy

People lined the streets to see Franklin D. Roosevelt's funeral procession down Constitution Avenue in Washington, D.C., on April 14, 1945.

was with him at his vacation cottage in Warm Springs, Georgia, on April 12, 1945, when he died from a sudden bleeding in the brain. Eleanor was at a charity event. She was called to the phone and given the sad news. "This was a terrible blow," she wrote.

She invited Vice President Harry S. Truman to the White House and told him that Franklin was dead. Truman would now become president. She asked, "Is there anything *we* can do for *you*? For you are the one in trouble now."

Then she flew to Georgia to bring Franklin's body back for funeral services. He was buried in the Rose Garden at Hyde Park. When she moved out of the White House, Eleanor told reporters, "The story is over." It wasn't.

An Honored Citizen of the World ∼

Unlike most First Ladies, Eleanor Roosevelt didn't leave public life when she left the White House. Nor did she accept the money usually given to widows of presidents. She chose to earn her own living. She wrote newspaper and magazine columns, gave radio and television talks, and lectures.

Eleanor also traveled around the globe visiting countries like Japan, India, Britain, Lebanon, and the Soviet

Union. World leaders welcomed her even though they did not always agree with American ideas.

Eleanor continued to work for equal rights for African Americans. She became a member of the Board of Directors of the National Association for the Advancement of Colored People (NAACP) in 1945.

Later that year, Eleanor accepted President Truman's offer to become a delegate to the General Assembly of the United Nations (UN). This was a new world organization that tried to solve the problems of its member nations.

Eleanor wrote in her newspaper column that she took on the job "because it seemed I might be able to use the experiences of a lifetime and make them valuable to my nation and to the people of the world. . . ." She also wrote that the other American delegates, all men, thought, "Ah, here's a safe spot for her—Committee Three. She can't do much harm there!"

The Third Committee of the General Assembly was not supposed to deal with disputes. It was meant to handle matters affecting people's knowledge, relationships, and the arts. However, it soon had to settle a dispute concerning refugees living in camps. The refugees did not want to be forced to return to their homelands, to live under governments they did not support. Those governments wanted them back. Eleanor defended the refugees' right to refuse to go home.

In 1946, President Truman asked Eleanor to serve on the Human Rights Commission of the General Assembly. Its members made her their chairperson. They had to decide how to protect all the world's peoples and help them live in freedom. It was a long, hard task because nations didn't always agree. Their ways of life were very different from one another. Two and a half years later (in December 1948) the General Assembly voted to approve The Universal Declaration of Human Rights. Member nations

Indian Prime Minister Jawaharlal Nehru and his wife met with Eleanor at Hyde Park in 1949. Many other world leaders came to Val-Kill to see her, including Soviet Prime Minister Nikita Khrushchev, Ethiopian Emperor Haile Selassie, and Yugoslavian Marshal Josip Tito.

promised to protect rights like freedom to travel, equality before the law, privacy, free education, ownership of property, and security in old age.

By now, the United States and the Soviet Union had become rivals. At home, Senator Joseph McCarthy of Wisconsin accused some people of supporting the Soviet Union, including Americans for Democratic Action (ADA). Eleanor helped found this group to improve life in the United States. Despite McCarthy's charges, ADA members were in fact patriotic citizens.

In 1952, Eleanor stopped working at the United Nations. Republican Dwight D. Eisenhower was elected president. Eleanor thought he should choose his own UN team. She went to work for the American Association of the United Nations (AAUN) in 1953. It promoted the work of the UN by giving lectures about UN programs around the country. She joined this group so that she could help " . . . to bring together all nations in an effort to maintain world peace."

Eleanor spent part of each year in New York and part at Hyde Park. In 1945, she and her children gave the house where Franklin grew up to the government. Eleanor decided to keep the land and buildings at Val-Kill. There they met with world leaders who came to visit her husband's grave.

Hyde Park in New York was Sara Roosevelt's home, not Eleanor's, even though Eleanor lived there for part of her life. Sara only had two easy chairs by the fire, one for herself and one for Franklin.

She also entertained her five children, their spouses, twenty grandchildren, thirteen great-grandchildren, and her many cousins there. On Christmas Day, they listened to her read Charles Dickens's *A Christmas Carol*. Every summer, she invited a hundred or so children from the Wiltwyck School for troubled boys. She gave them a picnic and read them stories from Rudyard Kipling's *Jungle Book*.

Eleanor never lost interest in American politics. She supported Governor Adlai E. Stevenson of Illinois when he ran for president. He lost to Dwight Eisenhower. Then in 1960 she backed Democratic candidate John F. Kennedy. President Kennedy made Eleanor a delegate to the United Nations again. He also invited her to lead the President's Commission on the Status of Women.

Eleanor with President John F. Kennedy. President Kennedy started the Peace Corps in 1961 to promote world peace and help developing countries. Eleanor also helped that mission by working on the Advisory Council of the Peace Corps.

"I sometimes think of quickly finishing up all the things I have to do, and then just not doing any more, but there always seem to be so many things to do," Eleanor said. One of those things was teaching students at Brandeis University in Massachusetts. She started at the age of seventy-five, but she was getting tired. At the age of seventy-eight, she complained, "I can't work. I don't understand it."

Eleanor went to the hospital for tests. She had a rare blood disease that could not be cured. On November 7, 1962, she died. She was buried beside her husband in the Rose Garden at Hyde Park.

Fala was one of the most famous White House pets. Franklin's cousin gave the dog to the president in 1940. Eleanor kept the Scottie after Franklin died and later raised one of Fala's puppies.

"To her the world was truly one world, and all its inhabitants members of one family," a European statesman wrote. Harry Truman probably had the same idea when he called her the "first lady of the world."

Time Line

1884	October 11	Birth of Anna Eleanor Roosevelt
1892	December 7	Death of Anna Hall Roosevelt, Eleanor's mother
1894	August 14	Death of Elliott Roosevelt, Eleanor's father
1905	March 17	Married to Franklin D. Roosevelt
1906	May 3	Birth of daughter Anna Eleanor
1907	December 23	Birth of son James
1909	March 18	Birth of (first) son Franklin Jr.
	November 8	Death of Franklin Jr.
1910	September 23	Birth of son Elliott
1914	August 17	Birth of (second) son Franklin Jr.
1916	March 13	Birth of son John
1927		Starts Val-Kill Industries and builds Val-Kill cottage on the Roosevelt estate
1928		Franklin is elected governor, but Eleanor continues teaching at the Todhunter School
1933		Becomes First Lady
1936		Starts newspaper column "My Day"
1941		Assistant Director of Office of Civilian Defense (OCD)
	September 7	Death of Sara Delano Roosevelt, Franklin's mother
	September 25	Death of Hall Roosevelt, Eleanor's brother
1942		Travels to Great Britain
1943–1944		Travels to the Pacific and the Caribbean, visiting American servicemen and Red Cross facilities
1945		Joins the Board of the National Association for the Advancement of Colored People (NAACP)
		Becomes a delegate to the United Nations (UN)
	April 12	Death of Franklin Delano Roosevelt
1947		Helps found Americans for Democratic Action (ADA)

1952		Resigns from the United Nations
1953		Joins American Association for the United Nations
1961		Becomes a delegate to the United Nations and chairperson of the Presidential Commission on the Status of Women
1962	November 7	Dies and is buried at Hyde Park

Bibliography

Boller, Paul F., Jr. *Presidential Wives: An Anecdotal History.* New York: Oxford University Press, 1988.

Burns, James MacGregor, and Susan Dunn. *The Three Roosevelts.* New York: Atlantic Monthly Press, 2001.

Caroli, Betty Boyd. *The Roosevelt Women.* New York: Basic Books, 1998.

Collier, Peter, and David Horowitz. *The Roosevelts: An American Saga.* New York: Simon & Schuster, 1994.

Cook, Blanche Wiesen. *Eleanor Roosevelt.* Vol. 1. New York: Penguin Books, 1993.

Glendon, Mary Ann. *A World Made New: Eleanor Roosevelt and the Universal Declaration of Human Rights.* New York: Random House, 2001.

Godwin, Doris Kearns. *No Ordinary Time.* New York: Simon & Schuster, 1994.

Hershan, Stella K. *The Candles She Lit: The Legacy of Eleanor Roosevelt.* Hyde Park, NY: Eleanor Roosevelt Center at Val-Kill, 2000.

Lash, Joseph P. *Eleanor and Franklin.* New York: W. W. Norton, 1971.

Lash, Joseph P. *Eleanor: The Years Alone.* New York: W. W. Norton, 1972.

Roosevelt, Eleanor. *The Autobiography of Eleanor Roosevelt.* New York: Da Capo Press, 1992.

Further Reading

Cooney, Barbara. *Eleanor.* New York: Viking Children's Book, 1996.

Freedman, Russell. *Eleanor Roosevelt: A Life of Discovery.* Boston: Houghton Mifflin, 1997.

Gottfried, Ted. *Eleanor Roosevelt: First Lady of the Twentieth Century.* Danbury, CT: Franklin Watts, 1997.

Kulling, Monica. *Eleanor Everywhere.* New York: Random House, 1999.

Ryan, Pam Muñoz. *Amelia and Eleanor Go For a Ride: Based on a True Story.* New York: Scholastic. 1999.

Santow, Dan. "Anna Eleanor Roosevelt: 1884–1962" in *Encyclopedia of First Ladies.* Danbury, CT: Children's Press, 1999.

INTERNET SITES ABOUT ELEANOR ROOSEVELT

Eleanor Roosevelt: American First Lady & Humanitarian 1884–1962
www.Lucidcafe.com/library/95oct/roosevel.html

PBS's The American Experience: Eleanor Roosevelt
www.pbs.org/wgbh/amex/eleanor

United Nations Universal Declaration of Human Rights 50th Anniversary 1948–1998: Eleanor Roosevelt Leads the Effort to Adopt the Universal Declaration of Human Rights
www.projectrespect.org/roosevelt.htm

The Eleanor Roosevelt Center at Val-Kill
www.ervk.org

Eleanor Roosevelt Historic Site (National Park Service)
www.nps.gov/elro/

FDR Library & Digital Archives K-12 Learning Center: Eleanor Roosevelt 1884–1962
www.fdrlibrary.marist.edu/bioer.html

Index

Page numbers in *italics* refer to illustrations.